Grade
3
Ages 8–9

Master Math at Home

Fractions

"Scan the QR code to help your child's learning at home."

 |

mastermathathome.com

How to use this book

Math — No Problem! created **Master Math at Home** to help children develop fluency in the subject and a rich understanding of core concepts.

Key features of the Master Math at Home books include:

- Carefully designed lessons that provide structure, but also allow flexibility in how they're used.

- Speech bubbles containing content designed to spark diverse conversations, with many discussion points that don't have obvious "right" or "wrong" answers.

- Rich illustrations that will guide children to a discussion of shapes and units of measurement, allowing them to make connections to the wider world around them.

- Exercises that allow a flexible approach and can be adapted to suit any child's cognitive or functional ability.

- Clearly laid-out pages that encourage children to practice a range of higher-order skills.

- A community of friendly and relatable characters who introduce each lesson and come along as your child progresses through the series.

You can see more guidance on how to use these books at mastermathathome.com.

We're excited to share all the ways you can learn math!

Copyright © 2022 Math — No Problem!

Math — No Problem!
mastermathathome.com
www.mathnoproblem.com
hello@mathnoproblem.com

First American Edition, 2022
Published in the United States by DK Publishing
1745 Broadway, 20th Floor, New York, NY 10019

22 23 24 25 26 10 9 8 7 6 5 4 3 2 1
002–327141–Nov/2022

This book was made with Forest Stewardship Council™ certified paper—one small step in DK's commitment to a sustainable future. For more information go to www.dk.com/our-green-pledge

All rights reserved. Without limiting the rights under the copyright reserved above, no part of this publication may be reproduced, stored in or introduced into a retrieval system, or transmitted, in any form, or by any means (electronic, mechanical, photocopying, recording, or otherwise), without the prior written permission of the copyright owner.
Published in Great Britain by Dorling Kindersley Limited

A catalog record for this book is available from the Library of Congress.
ISBN: 978-0-7440-5195-7
Printed and bound in China

For the curious
www.dk.com

Acknowledgments

The publisher would like to thank the authors and consultants Andy Psarianos, Judy Hornigold, Adam Gifford, Dr. Wong Khoon Yoong, and Dr. Anne Hermanson.

The Castledown typeface has been used with permission from the Colophon Foundry.

Contents

	Page
Counting in Tenths	4
Adding Like Fractions (Part 1)	6
Adding Like Fractions (Part 2)	8
Number Pairs	10
Subtracting Like Fractions	12
Equivalent Fractions	14
Equivalent Fractions on a Number Line	16
Equivalent Fractions Using Multiplication	18
Finding Equivalent Fractions (Part 1)	20
Finding Equivalent Fractions (Part 2)	22
Comparing Unit Fractions	24
Comparing Unlike Fractions	26
Subtracting Fractions (Part 1)	28
Subtracting Fractions (Part 2)	30
Finding Part of a Set (Part 1)	32
Finding Part of a Set (Part 2)	34
Sharing 1	36
Sharing More Than 1	38
Sharing More Than 1 Using Improper Fractions	40
Review and Challenge	42
Answers	46

Ruby   Elliott   Amira   Charles   Lulu   Sam   Oak   Holly   Ravi   Emma   Jacob   Hannah

Counting in Tenths

Lesson 1

Starter

What fraction of the rectangle is shaded?

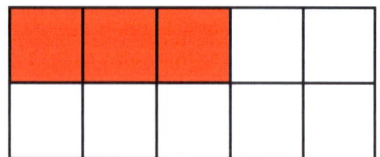

The whole rectangle is divided into 10 equal parts.

Each part is called one tenth.

Example

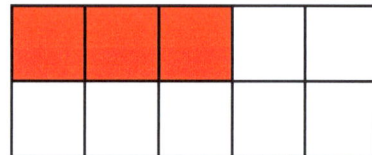

3 tenths of the rectangle is shaded and 7 tenths of the rectangle is not shaded.

$\frac{3}{10}$ of the rectangle is shaded.

We write 3 tenths as $\frac{3}{10}$.

We can also show 3 tenths on a number line.

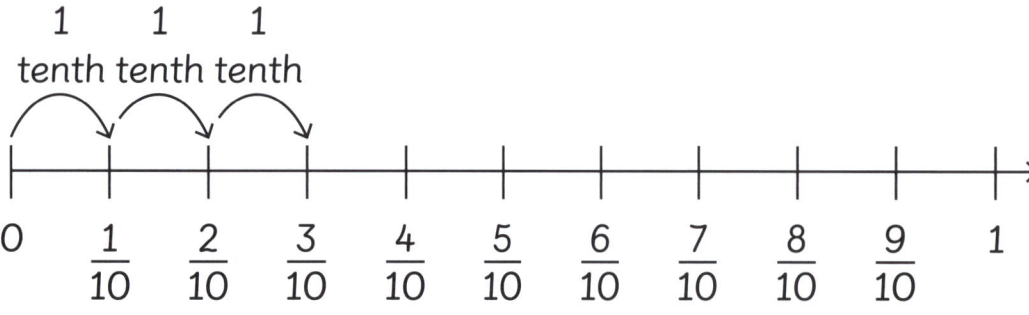

Practice

1 What fraction of the rectangle is shaded?

(a) 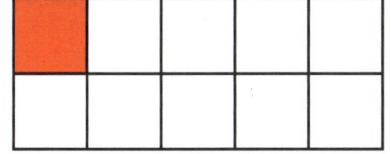 (b)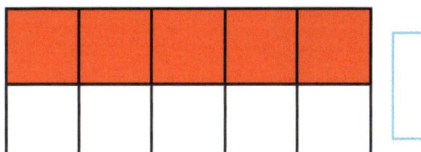

2 What fraction of each shape is shaded?

(a) 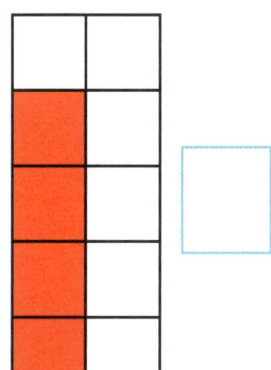 (b)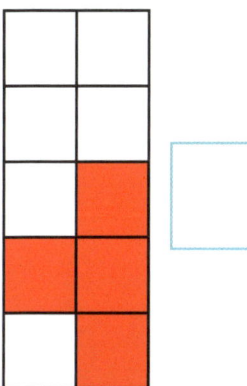

(c) 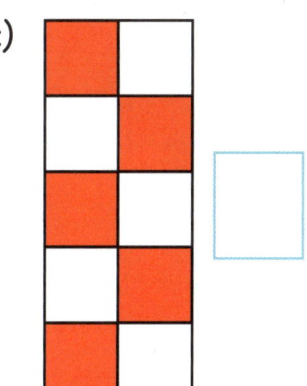 (d)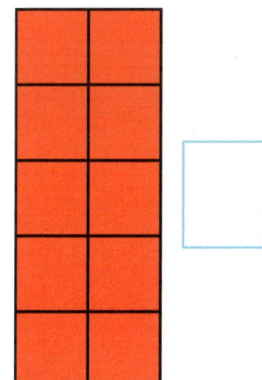

(e) 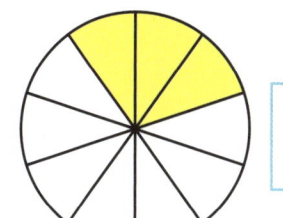 (f) 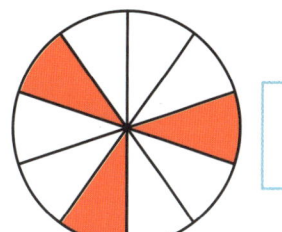 (g)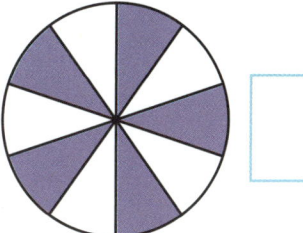

3 Fill in the blanks.

0   $\frac{1}{10}$ $\frac{2}{10}$ 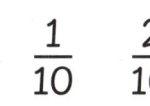    $\frac{5}{10}$     $\frac{8}{10}$ ⬜   1

Adding Like Fractions (Part 1)

Lesson 2

Starter

Charles and Emma cut a sushi roll into 5 equal pieces.

 I ate 1 piece. 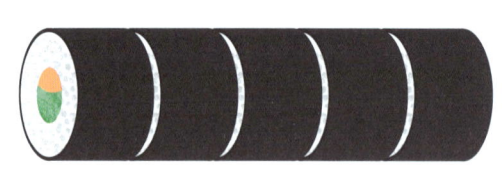 I ate 2 pieces.

What fraction of the sushi roll did they eat?

Example

 Each piece is 1 fifth of the sushi roll.

 Charles ate 1 fifth of the sushi roll.

 Emma ate 2 fifths of the sushi roll.

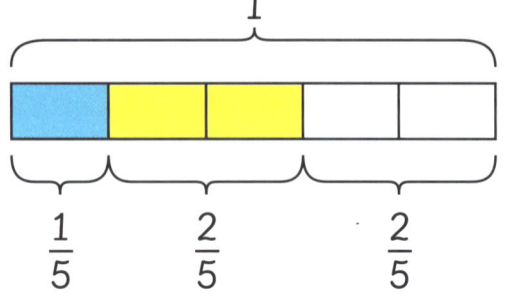

$1 = \frac{5}{5}$

1 fifth + 2 fifths = 3 fifths
$\frac{1}{5} + \frac{2}{5} = \frac{3}{5}$

There are 2 pieces or $\frac{2}{5}$ left over.

Charles and Emma ate $\frac{3}{5}$ of the sushi roll.

Practice

1 Add.

(a) $\frac{1}{5} + \frac{3}{5} =$ ☐

(b) $\frac{2}{5} + \frac{2}{5} =$ ☐

(c) $\frac{1}{9} + \frac{7}{9} =$ ☐

(d) $\frac{2}{7} + \frac{2}{7} =$ ☐

(e) $\frac{1}{4} + \frac{3}{4} =$ ☐

(f) $\frac{3}{6} + \frac{3}{6} =$ ☐

2 Write four pairs of fractions that add up to 1.

(a) ☐ + ☐ = 1

(b) ☐ + ☐ = 1

(c) ☐ + ☐ = 1

(d) ☐ + ☐ = 1

3 Add.

(a) $\frac{1}{4} + \frac{1}{4} + \frac{1}{4} =$ ☐

(b) $\frac{1}{3} + \frac{1}{3} + \frac{1}{3} =$ ☐

(c) $\frac{1}{5} + \frac{2}{5} + \frac{1}{5} =$ ☐

(d) $\frac{1}{7} + \frac{2}{7} + \frac{3}{7} =$ ☐

Adding Like Fractions (Part 2)

Lesson 3

Starter

 I ate $\frac{2}{6}$ of the pie.

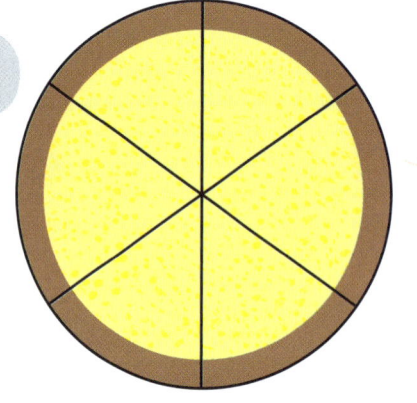

I ate $\frac{3}{6}$ of the pie.

How much of the pie did the friends eat in total?

Example

Add $\frac{2}{6}$ and $\frac{3}{6}$.

 $\frac{2}{6}$

 $\frac{3}{6}$

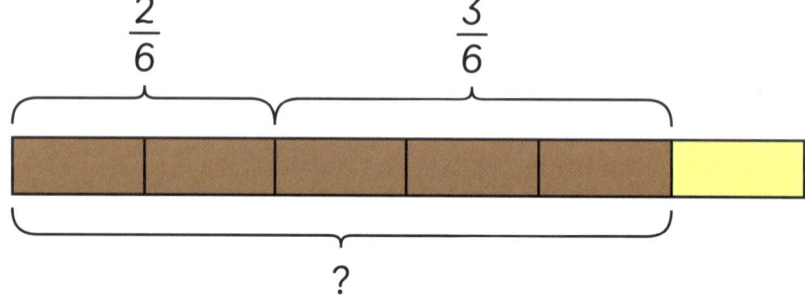

$\frac{2}{6} + \frac{3}{6} = \frac{5}{6}$

The friends ate $\frac{5}{6}$ of the pie in total.

8

Practice

1 Add and fill in the blanks.

(a)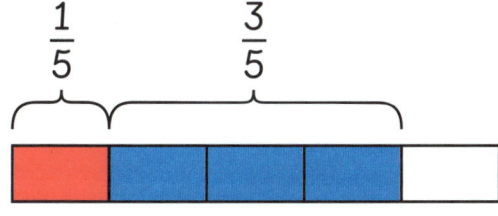
$\frac{1}{5} + \frac{3}{5} = \boxed{}$

(b)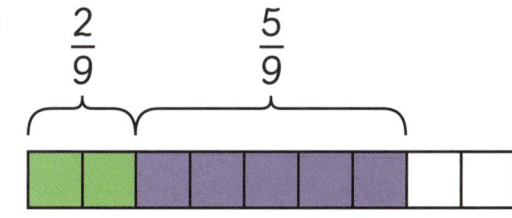
$\frac{2}{9} + \frac{5}{9} = \boxed{}$

(c)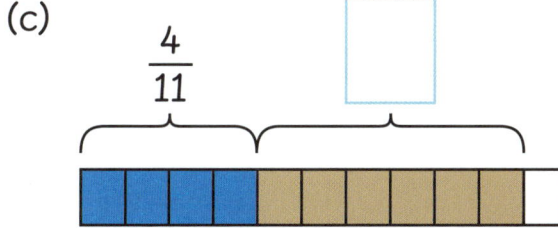
$\frac{4}{11} + \boxed{} = \boxed{}$

2 (a) $\frac{1}{4} + \frac{2}{4} = \boxed{}$ (b) $\frac{2}{9} + \frac{4}{9} = \boxed{}$

(c) $\frac{1}{6} + \frac{5}{6} = \boxed{}$ (d) $\frac{1}{15} + \frac{4}{15} = \boxed{}$

(e) $\frac{3}{7} + \frac{2}{7} = \boxed{}$ (f) $\frac{4}{15} + \frac{7}{15} = \boxed{}$

Number Pairs

Lesson 4

Starter

 I take 7 eighths of the chocolate bar.

 I take 1 eighth of the chocolate bar.

How many ways can Oak and Ruby share the 8 pieces of the chocolate bar?

Example

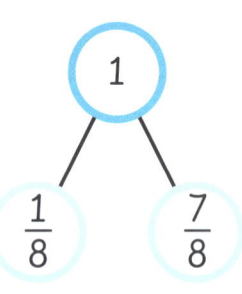

Oak	Ruby
$\frac{1}{8}$	$\frac{7}{8}$
$\frac{2}{8}$	$\frac{6}{8}$
$\frac{3}{8}$	$\frac{5}{8}$
$\frac{4}{8}$	$\frac{4}{8}$
$\frac{5}{8}$	$\frac{3}{8}$
$\frac{6}{8}$	$\frac{2}{8}$
$\frac{7}{8}$	$\frac{1}{8}$

 I can make a table.

 Each piece is 1 eighth of the chocolate bar.

There are 7 different ways that Oak and Ruby can share the eight pieces of the chocolate bar.

10

Practice

1 Match.

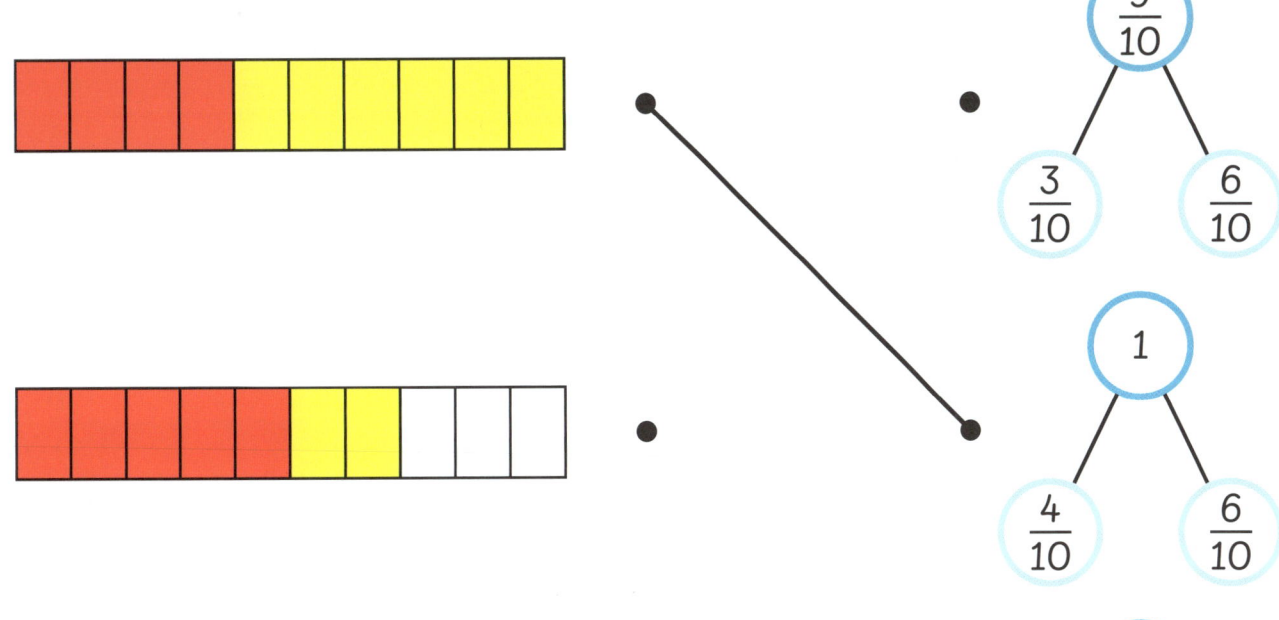

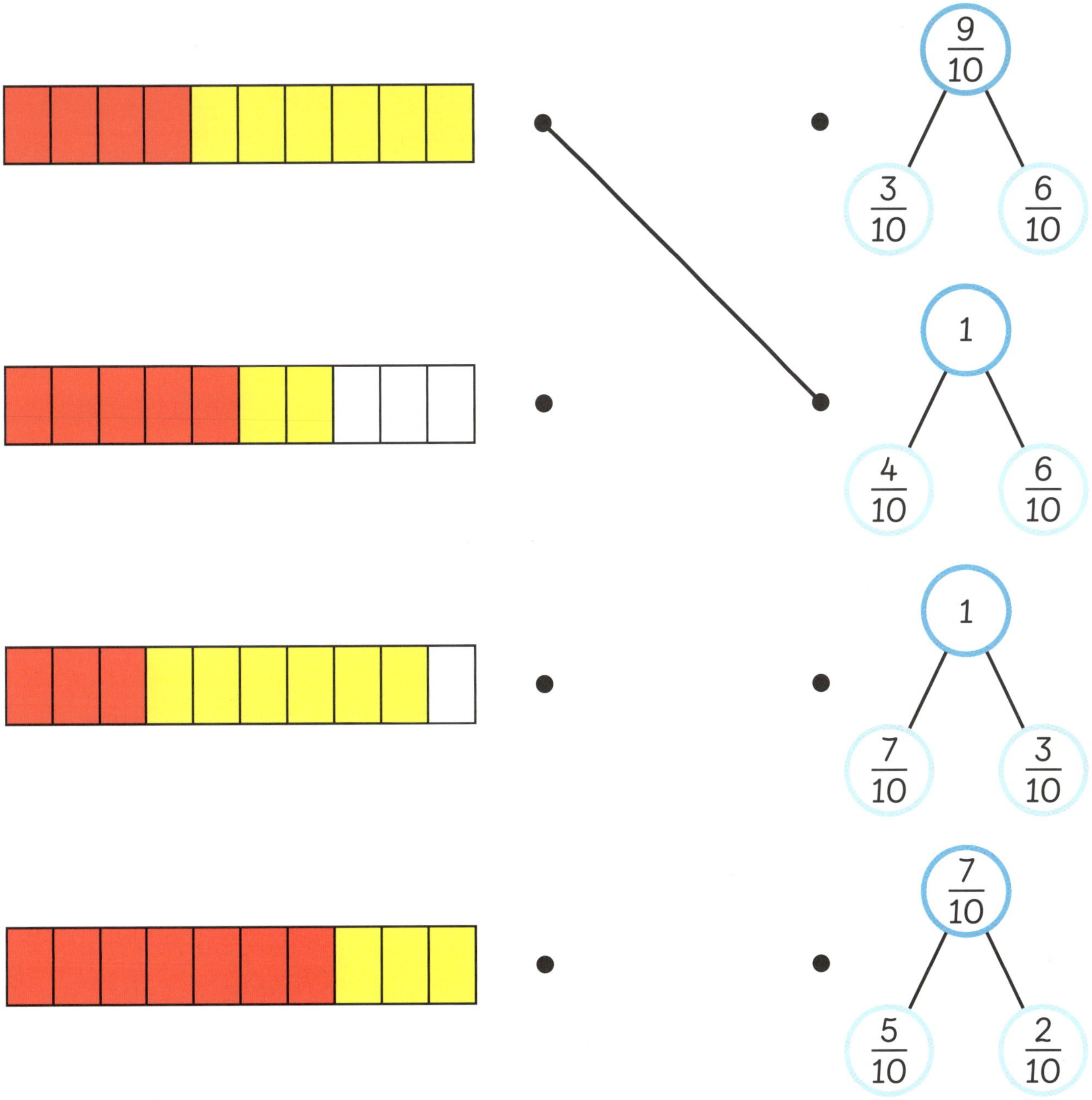

2 Fill in the blanks.

(a)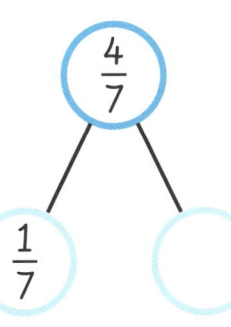

(b)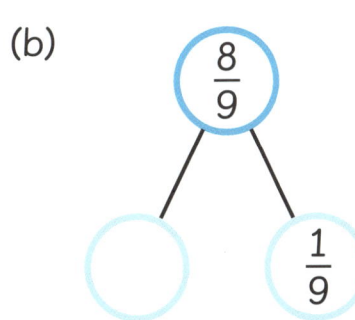

(c)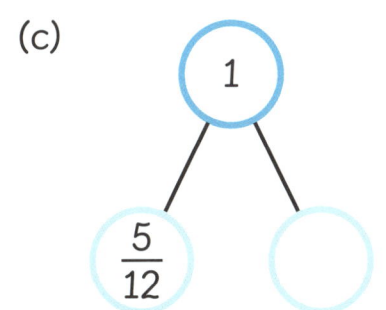

Subtracting Like Fractions

Lesson 5

Starter

A jelly roll is cut into 6 equal pieces.
Elliott takes 1 piece and then Hannah takes 2 pieces.
How much of the jelly roll is left?

Example

The roll was cut into 6 equal pieces. Each piece is 1 sixth.

Elliott has taken 1 piece and Hannah is taking 2 pieces.

There are 3 pieces left.

After Hannah takes 2 pieces, there is $\frac{3}{6}$ of the jelly roll left.

Practice

1 Fill in the blanks.

(a)

$\frac{3}{5} - \frac{1}{5} = \boxed{}$

(b)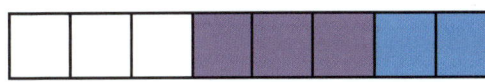

$\frac{5}{8} - \frac{2}{8} = \boxed{}$

(c)

$\frac{4}{7} - \boxed{} = \frac{1}{7}$

(d)

$\boxed{} - \frac{3}{12} = \boxed{}$

2 Charles spends $\frac{1}{4}$ of his money on a pencil case.

He then spends $\frac{2}{3}$ of his remaining money on some books.

What fraction of the money he started with does he have left?

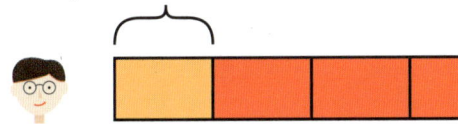

pencil case

Charles has $\boxed{}$ of the money he started with left.

Equivalent Fractions

Lesson 6

Starter

Holly folds a strip of paper into 4 equal parts and shades 1 part.

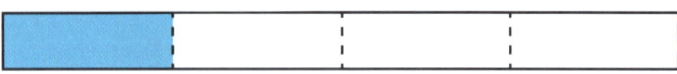

What happens if Holly keeps folding the paper?

I shaded $\frac{1}{4}$ of the strip of paper.

Example

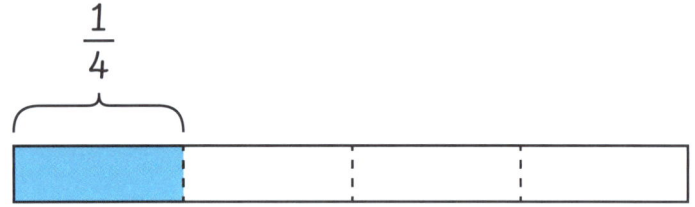

This strip of paper is folded into quarters.

Holly folds the strip of paper again.

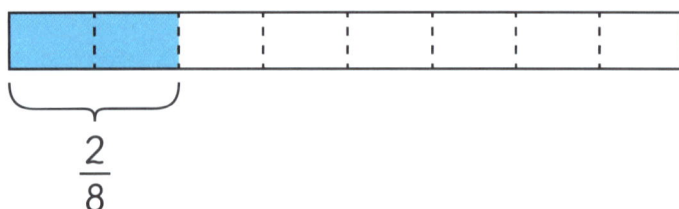

The same amount of paper is shaded, but there are more parts.

Now the strip of paper is in 8 parts. It is folded into eighths.

 ← numerator
← denominator

Equivalent fractions have different numerators and denominators but have an equal value.

Practice

1 Fill in the blanks.

(a)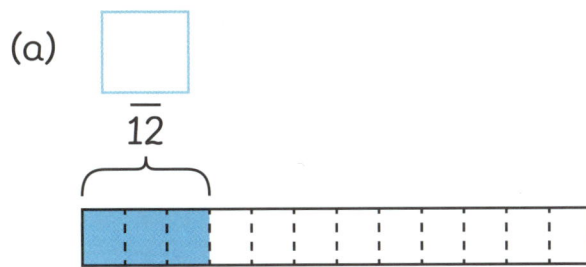

(b)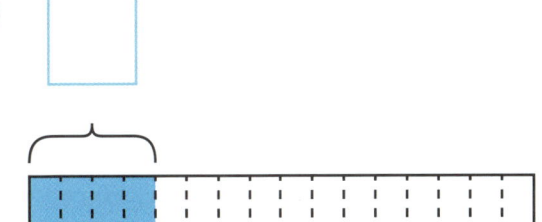

2 Fill in the blanks.

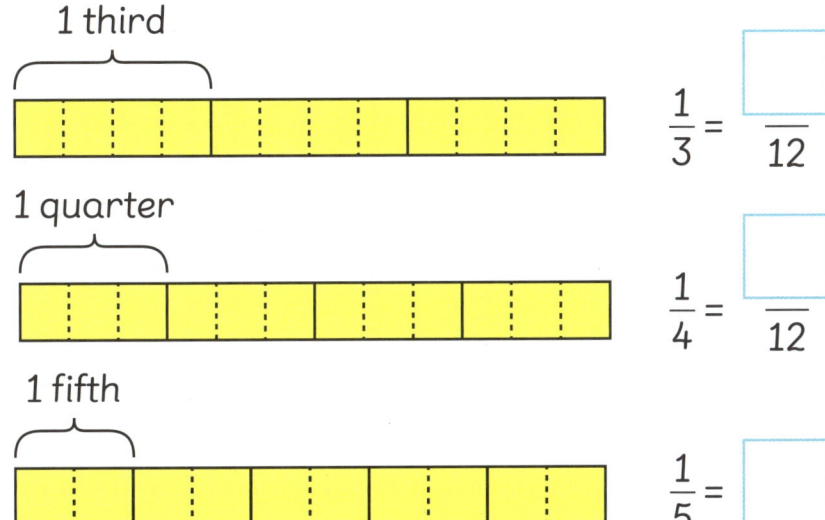

$\frac{1}{3} = \frac{\square}{12}$

$\frac{1}{4} = \frac{\square}{12}$

$\frac{1}{5} = \square$

3 Oak, Ruby, and Holly all ordered equal-size pizzas. They each ate $\frac{1}{2}$ of their pizzas. Oak ate 3 slices of her pizza, Ruby ate 4 slices of her pizza, and Holly ate 2 slices of her pizza.

What fraction of a whole pizza were Oak's, Ruby's, and Holly's slices?

Oak's slices were ☐ of a pizza, Ruby's slices were ☐ of a pizza, and Holly's slices were ☐ of a pizza.

Equivalent Fractions on a Number Line

Lesson 7

Starter

Four friends are learning how to tie knots on a sailing course. The sailor gives them a long piece of rope and tells them they each need 2 equal-size pieces of rope. How much rope does each friend get?

Example

First, we cut the rope into 2 pieces.

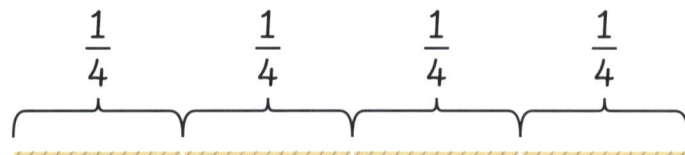

We then cut each half into 2 equal-size pieces.

Each half is now $\frac{2}{4}$ of the original rope.

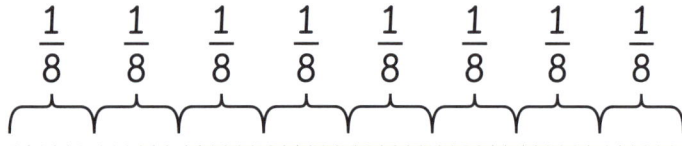

Each friend gets $\frac{1}{4}$ of the rope.

Each friend needs 2 pieces of rope. They can cut their quarter into 2 pieces. Each quarter becomes $\frac{2}{8}$.

 We can use a number line to find equivalent fractions.

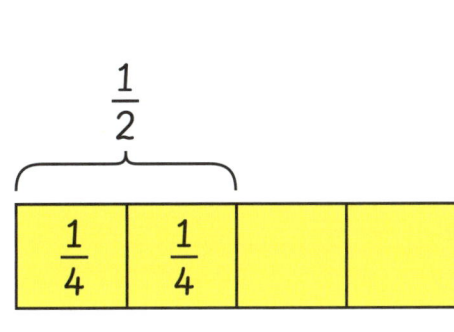
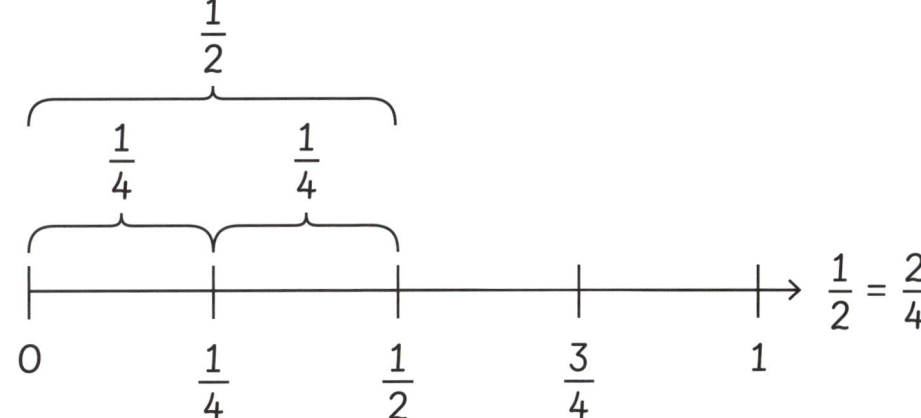

$\dfrac{1}{2} = \dfrac{2}{4}$

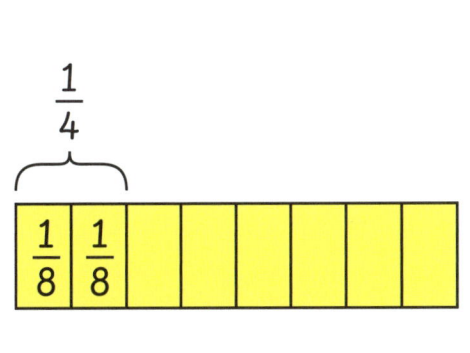
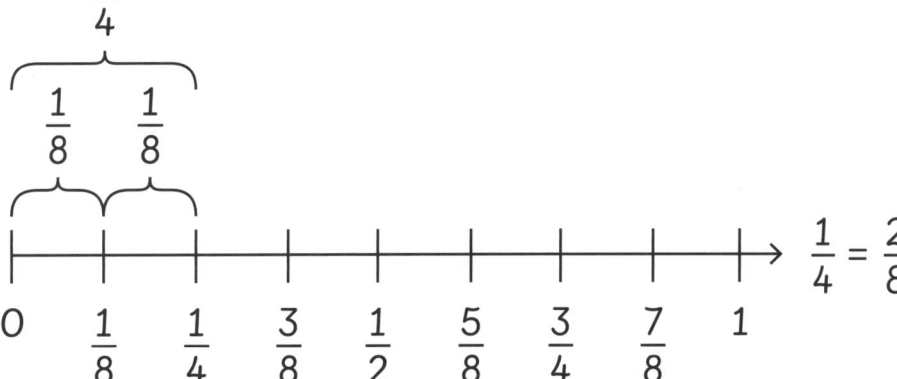

$\dfrac{1}{4} = \dfrac{2}{8}$

Practice

1 Mark $\dfrac{1}{3}$ and $\dfrac{1}{2}$ on the number line.

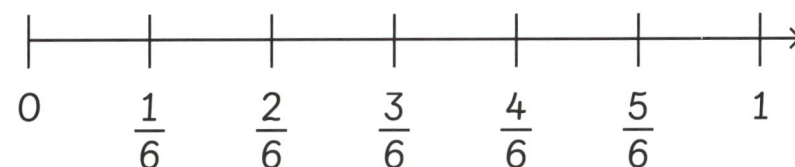

2 Mark $\dfrac{1}{4}$ and $\dfrac{3}{6}$ on the number line.

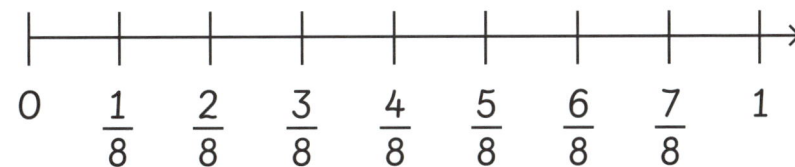

17

Equivalent Fractions Using Multiplication

Lesson 8

Starter

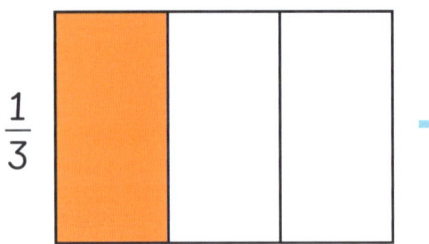  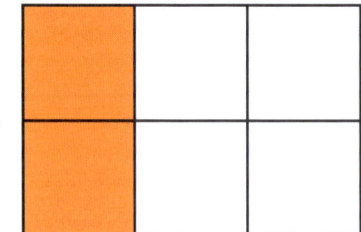

$\frac{1}{3}$ and $\frac{2}{6}$ are equivalent fractions. Are there other fractions equivalent to $\frac{1}{3}$?

Example

This is $\frac{1}{3}$.

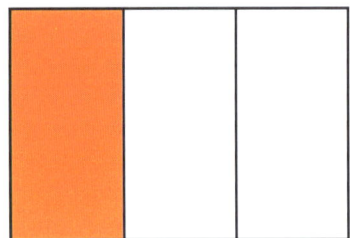

When the shaded part becomes 2 equal parts, each part is $\frac{1}{6}$.

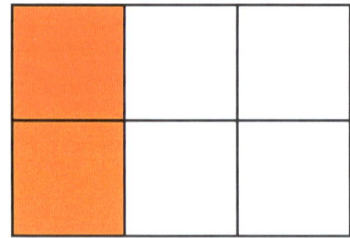

$\frac{1}{3} = \frac{2}{6}$

When the shaded part becomes 3 equal parts, each part is $\frac{1}{9}$.

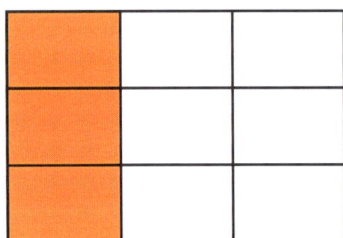

$\frac{1}{3} = \frac{3}{9}$

When the shaded part becomes 4 equal parts, each part is $\frac{1}{12}$.

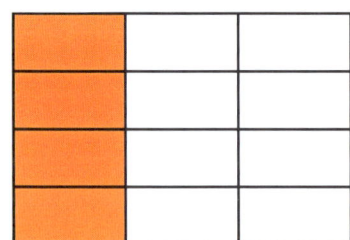

$\frac{1}{3} = \frac{4}{12}$

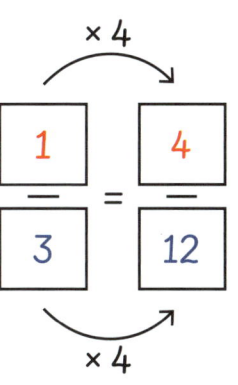

Practice

1 Find the missing numerators.

(a)

$\dfrac{3}{5} = \dfrac{\Box}{10}$

(b)

$\dfrac{3}{4} = \dfrac{\Box}{8}$

(c) $\dfrac{2}{7} = \dfrac{\Box}{14}$

(d) $\dfrac{5}{6} = \dfrac{\Box}{12}$

2 Fill in the blanks.

(a) ×□

$\dfrac{3}{4} = \dfrac{6}{\Box}$

×□

(b) ×□

$\dfrac{2}{5} = \dfrac{\Box}{15}$

×□

19

Finding Equivalent Fractions (Part 1)

Lesson 9

Starter

Lulu and Sam each have the same tray of lasagna.
Lulu cuts her lasagna into 4 equal-size pieces.
Sam cuts his lasagna into 8 equal-size pieces.

I took 1 piece.

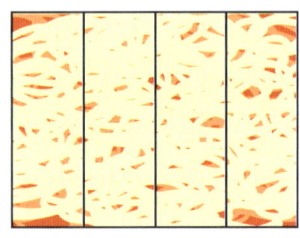

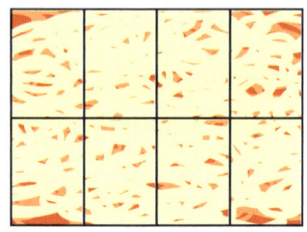

I took 2 pieces.

Have they both taken the same amount?

Example

$\frac{1}{4}$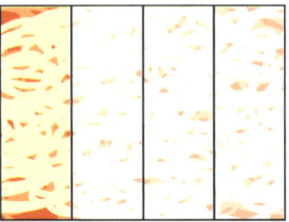

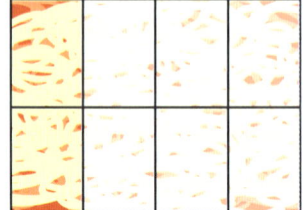 $\frac{2}{8}$

 Are $\frac{1}{4}$ and $\frac{2}{8}$ equivalent fractions?

$$\overset{\times 2}{\frac{1}{4} = \frac{2}{8}}$$

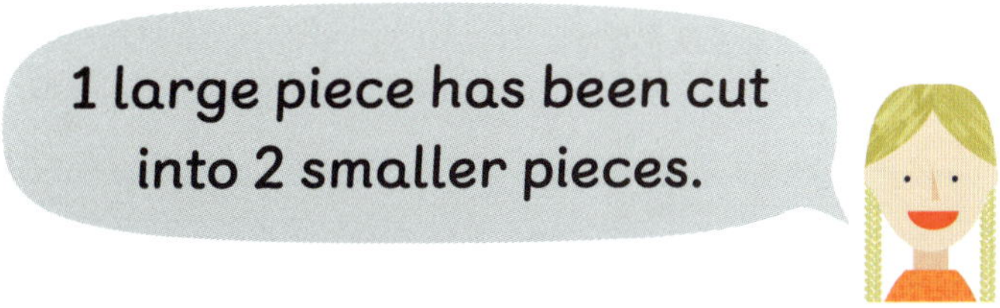

1 large piece has been cut into 2 smaller pieces.

$$\underset{\times 2}{\frac{1}{4} = \frac{2}{8}}$$

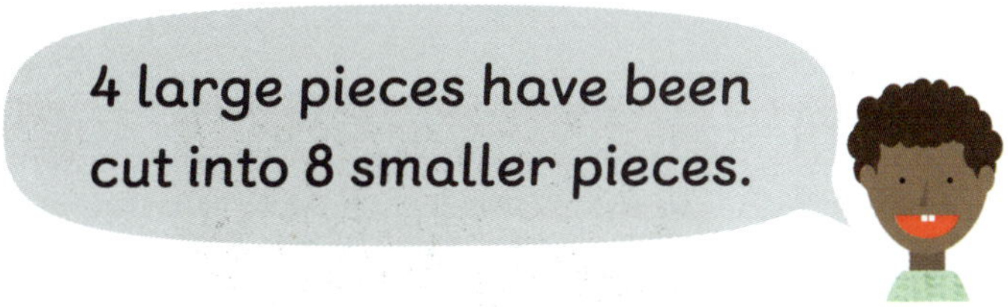

4 large pieces have been cut into 8 smaller pieces.

$\frac{1}{4}$ and $\frac{2}{8}$ are equivalent fractions.

Lulu and Sam have taken the same amount of lasagna.

Practice

1 Shade the bars and fill in the blanks.

(a) $\frac{1}{2} = \frac{\Box}{8}$

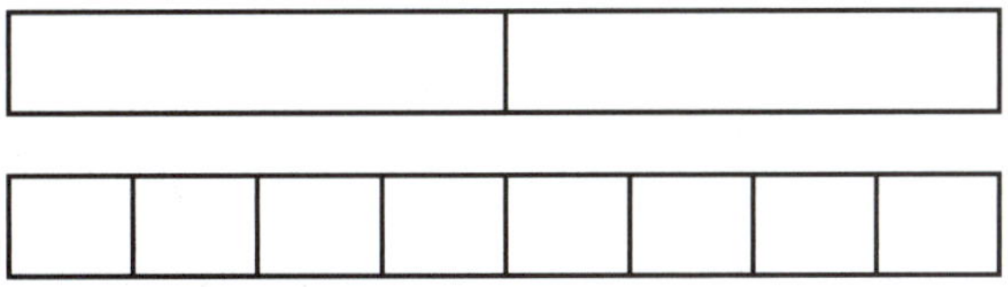

(b) $\frac{3}{4} = \frac{\Box}{8}$

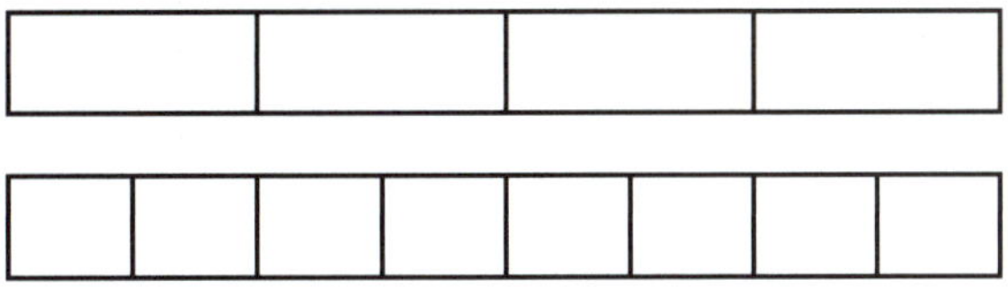

2 Fill in the blanks.

(a) $\overset{\times \Box}{\underset{\times \Box}{\frac{1}{5} = \frac{\Box}{10}}}$

(b) $\overset{\times \Box}{\underset{\times \Box}{\frac{3}{4} = \frac{\Box}{12}}}$

Finding Equivalent Fractions (Part 2)

Lesson 10

Starter

Can you see the pattern in these fractions?

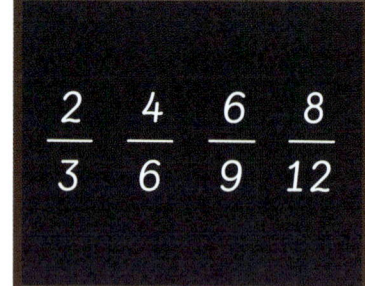

$\frac{2}{3} \quad \frac{4}{6} \quad \frac{6}{9} \quad \frac{8}{12}$

Are they equivalent fractions?

Example

When we make 2 equal parts into 4 equal parts, we also make 3 equal parts into 6 equal parts. We can use multiplication to help us find equivalent fractions.

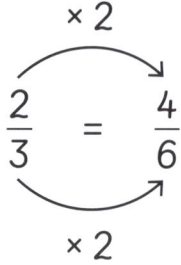

$\frac{2}{3} = \frac{4}{6}$ (× 2)

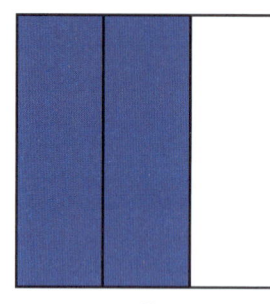

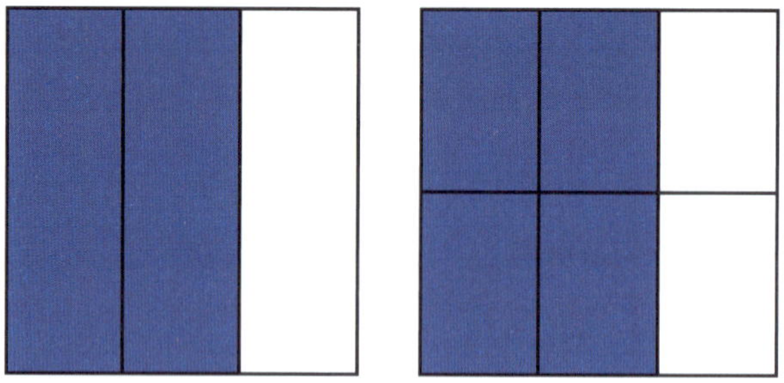

$\frac{2}{3} = \frac{4}{6}$

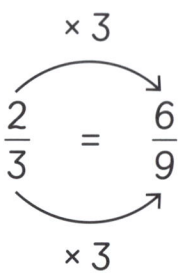

$\frac{2}{3} = \frac{6}{9}$ (× 3)

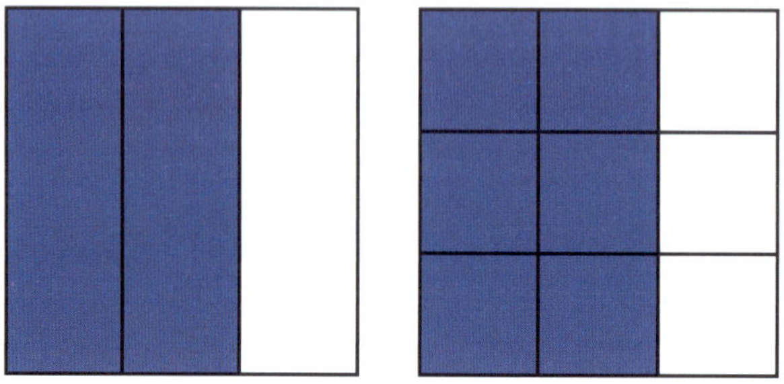

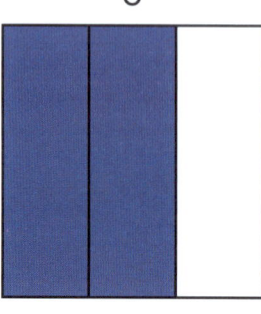

$\frac{2}{3} = \frac{6}{9}$

When we make 4 equal parts into 2 equal parts, we also make 6 equal parts into 3 equal parts. We can use division to help us simplify a fraction.

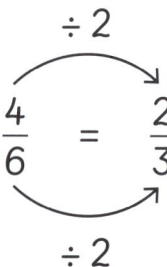

$\frac{4}{6} = \frac{2}{3}$ (÷ 2)

Practice

1 Fill in the blanks.

(a)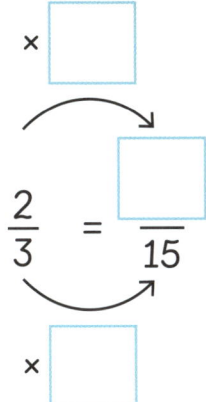

(b)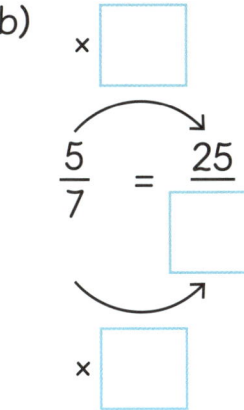

(c)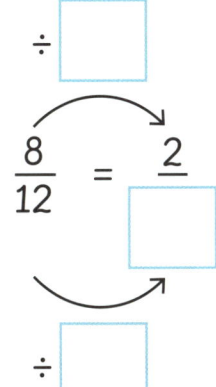

(d)
```
    ÷ □
  ┌───┐
  9    □
 ── = ──
 15    5
  └───┘
    ÷ □
```

2 Write each fraction in its simplest form.

(a) $\frac{15}{25} = \square$

(b) $\frac{15}{50} = \square$

(c) $\frac{5}{15} = \square$

(d) $\frac{50}{60} = \square$

(e) $\frac{12}{16} = \square$

(f) $\frac{8}{24} = \square$

The simplest form is the equivalent fraction with the smallest numbers.

23

Comparing Unit Fractions

Lesson 11

Starter

Ravi drank $\frac{1}{3}$ of his glass of juice.

Holly drank $\frac{1}{5}$ of her glass of juice.

Who drank more juice?

Example

Compare $\frac{1}{3}$ and $\frac{1}{5}$.

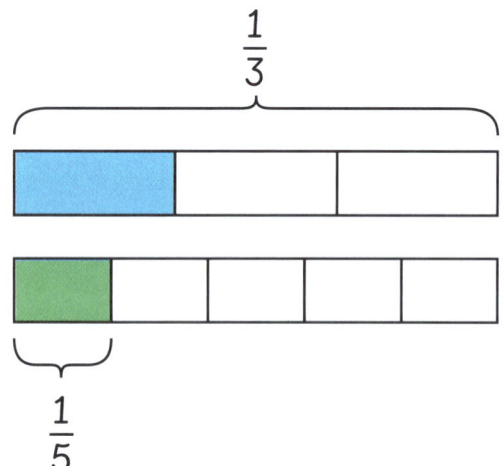

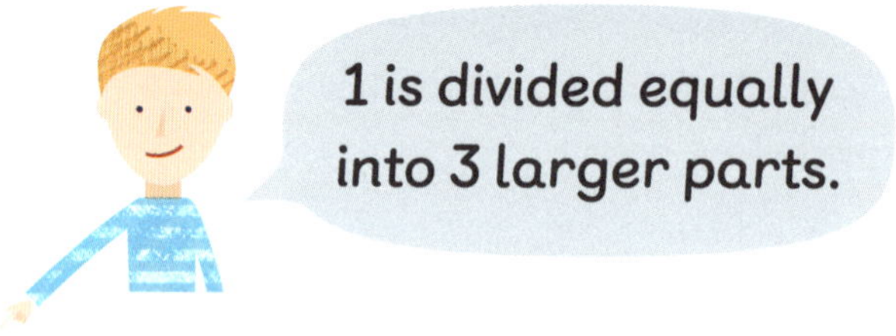

1 is divided equally into 3 larger parts.

1 is divided equally into 5 smaller parts.

Ravi's part is greater than Holly's part.

1 third is greater than 1 fifth.

$\frac{1}{3} > \frac{1}{5}$

Ravi drank more juice than Holly drank.

Practice

1 Fill in the blanks.

(a) Compare $\frac{1}{5}$ and $\frac{1}{7}$.

$\frac{1}{5}$

$\frac{1}{7}$

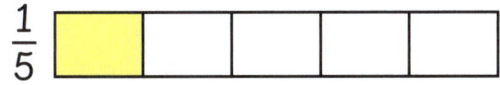

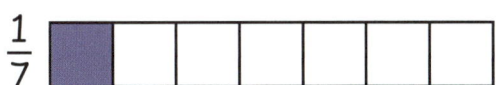

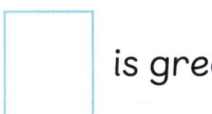

____ is greater than ____.

(b) Compare $\frac{1}{11}$ and $\frac{1}{9}$.

$\frac{1}{11}$

$\frac{1}{9}$

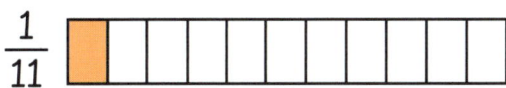

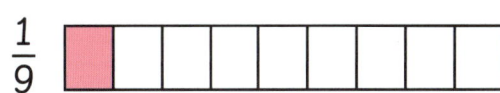

____ is smaller than ____.

2 Compare the fractions using > or <.

(a) $\frac{1}{8}$ ____ $\frac{1}{5}$

(b) $\frac{1}{2}$ ____ $\frac{1}{10}$

(c) $\frac{1}{3}$ ____ $\frac{1}{6}$

(d) $\frac{1}{9}$ ____ $\frac{1}{7}$

(e) $\frac{1}{2}$ ____ $\frac{1}{3}$

(f) $\frac{1}{5}$ ____ $\frac{1}{3}$

3 Put these fractions in order from smallest to greatest.

$\frac{1}{12}$ $\frac{1}{5}$ $\frac{1}{2}$ $\frac{1}{10}$

____, ____, ____, ____

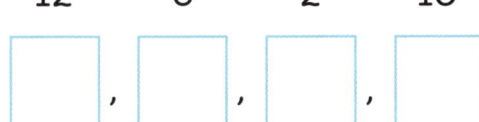

Comparing Unlike Fractions

Lesson 12

Starter

Oak and Ruby are reading the same book.

Oak has read $\frac{5}{6}$ of the book.

Ruby has read $\frac{5}{8}$ of the book.

Who has read more?

Example

Which is greater, $\frac{5}{6}$ or $\frac{5}{8}$?

1

| $\frac{1}{6}$ | $\frac{1}{6}$ | $\frac{1}{6}$ | $\frac{1}{6}$ | $\frac{1}{6}$ | $\frac{1}{6}$ |

| $\frac{1}{8}$ | $\frac{1}{8}$ | $\frac{1}{8}$ | $\frac{1}{8}$ | $\frac{1}{8}$ | $\frac{1}{8}$ | $\frac{1}{8}$ | $\frac{1}{8}$ |

$\frac{5}{6}$ is greater than $\frac{5}{8}$.

Oak has read more of the book than Ruby has.

$\frac{5}{6} > \frac{5}{8}$

Practice

1 Fill in the blanks.

(a) Compare $\frac{3}{7}$ and $\frac{3}{10}$.

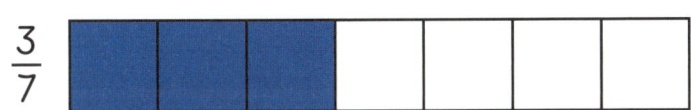

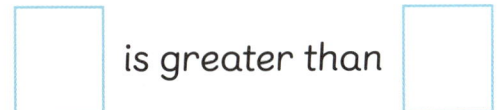 is greater than .

(b) Compare $\frac{9}{11}$ and $\frac{7}{10}$.

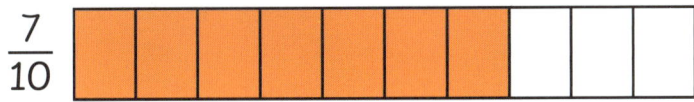

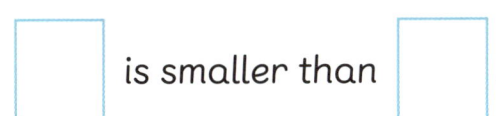 is smaller than .

2 Compare the fractions using >, <, or =.

(a) $\frac{2}{5}$ ☐ $\frac{2}{7}$ (b) $\frac{3}{7}$ ☐ $\frac{3}{4}$

(c) $\frac{7}{8}$ ☐ $\frac{7}{9}$ (d) $\frac{8}{9}$ ☐ $\frac{7}{8}$

(e) $\frac{10}{11}$ ☐ $\frac{8}{10}$ (f) $\frac{8}{8}$ ☐ $\frac{9}{9}$

Subtracting Fractions (Part 1)

Lesson 13

Starter

I will take 1 chocolate.

What fraction of the box of chocolates is left after Jacob takes 1 piece?

Example

Each piece is $\frac{1}{6}$ of the box of chocolates.

This is $\frac{5}{6}$ of the box of chocolates.

Jacob takes $\frac{1}{6}$ of the box of chocolates.

$\frac{5}{6} - \frac{1}{6} = \frac{4}{6}$

$\frac{4}{6} = \frac{2}{3}$

We can simplify $\frac{4}{6}$.

$\frac{2}{3}$ of the box of chocolates is left.

28

Practice

1 Subtract and simplify.

(a) $\dfrac{7}{8} - \dfrac{1}{8} = \boxed{} = \boxed{}$

(b) $\dfrac{7}{8} - \dfrac{3}{8} = \boxed{} = \boxed{}$

(c) $\dfrac{9}{10} - \dfrac{3}{10} = \boxed{} = \boxed{}$

(d) $\dfrac{5}{9} - \dfrac{2}{9} = \boxed{} = \boxed{}$

2 Subtract and simplify.

(a) $\dfrac{5}{6} - \dfrac{2}{6} = \boxed{} = \boxed{}$

(b) $\dfrac{11}{12} - \dfrac{2}{12} = \boxed{} = \boxed{}$

(c) $\dfrac{13}{15} - \dfrac{8}{15} = \boxed{} = \boxed{}$

(d) $\dfrac{7}{10} - \dfrac{2}{10} = \boxed{} = \boxed{}$

3 Answer the question in four different ways.

(a) $\dfrac{\boxed{}}{8} - \dfrac{\boxed{}}{8} = \dfrac{4}{8} = \dfrac{1}{2}$

(b) $\dfrac{\boxed{}}{8} - \dfrac{\boxed{}}{8} = \dfrac{4}{8} = \dfrac{1}{2}$

(c) $\dfrac{\boxed{}}{8} - \dfrac{\boxed{}}{8} = \dfrac{4}{8} = \dfrac{1}{2}$

(d) $\dfrac{\boxed{}}{8} - \dfrac{\boxed{}}{8} = \dfrac{4}{8} = \dfrac{1}{2}$

Subtracting Fractions (Part 2)

Lesson 14

Starter

Ravi uses $\frac{1}{4}$ of the construction paper.

What fraction of the construction paper is left?

Example

The construction paper is divided into quarters.

Ravi uses $\frac{1}{4}$ of the construction paper.

Subtract $\frac{1}{4}$ from $\frac{4}{4}$.

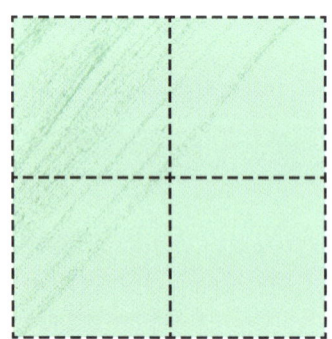

$1 = \frac{4}{4}$

$\frac{4}{4} = 1$ whole

$\frac{4}{4} - \frac{1}{4} = \frac{3}{4}$

$\frac{3}{4}$ of the construction paper is left.

Practice

1 Subtract.

(a) $1 - \frac{1}{3} = \square$

(b) $1 - \frac{2}{5} = \square$

(c) $1 - \frac{5}{6} = \square$

(d) $1 - \frac{3}{7} = \square$

2 Subtract and simplify.

(a) $1 - \frac{2}{8} = \square = \square$

(b) $1 - \frac{3}{9} = \square = \square$

(c) $1 - \frac{2}{10} = \square = \square$

(d) $1 - \frac{3}{6} = \square = \square$

3 Fill in the blanks.

(a) $1 - \frac{\square}{6} = \frac{4}{6} = \frac{2}{3}$

(b) $1 - \frac{\square}{10} = \frac{\square}{10} = \frac{1}{2}$

(c) $1 - \frac{\square}{4} = \frac{1}{2}$

Finding Part of a Set (Part 1)

Lesson 15

Starter

Ruby and Charles share this bag of apples equally.
How many apples do they each get?
How many ways can the apples be shared?

Example

$\frac{1}{2}$ of 8 apples = 4 apples

Ruby and Charles get 4 apples each.

8 ÷ 2 = 4

Can the apples be shared equally between 4 children?

$\frac{1}{4}$ of 8 apples = 2 apples

8 ÷ 4 = 2

Can the apples be shared equally between 8 children?

$\frac{1}{8}$ of 8 apples = 1 apple

8 ÷ 8 = 1

Practice

1 Fill in the blanks.

(a) Circle the cookies to show 4 equal groups.

$\frac{1}{4}$ of 16 cookies = ☐ cookies

(b) Circle the pears to show 3 equal groups.

$\frac{1}{3}$ of 15 pears = ☐ pears

2 Draw ☐ to help you find part of the set.

(a) | ☐ ☐ ☐ | ☐ ☐ ☐ | ☐ ☐ ☐ | ☐ ☐ ☐ |

$\frac{1}{4}$ of 12 pineapples = ☐ pineapples

(b) | | | | | |

$\frac{1}{5}$ of 20 balls = ☐ balls

(c) | | | |

$\frac{1}{3}$ of 18 children = ☐ children

33

Finding Part of a Set (Part 2)

Lesson 16

Starter

Lulu uses $\frac{3}{4}$ of the box of eggs to make cakes.

How many eggs does Lulu use to make the cakes?

Example

Start by finding $\frac{1}{4}$ of the eggs.

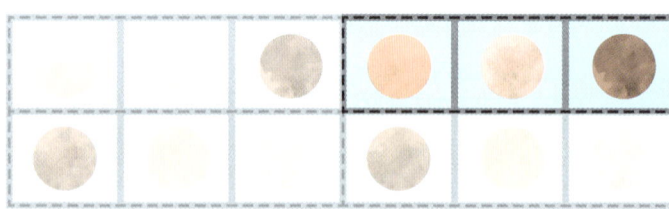

$\frac{1}{4}$ of 12 eggs = 3 eggs

$\frac{3}{4}$ of 12 eggs = 3 × 3 eggs
$\phantom{\frac{3}{4} \text{ of 12 eggs }}$ = 9 eggs

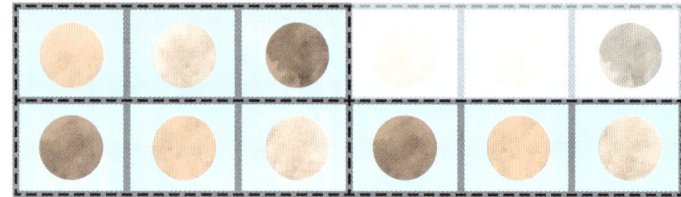

$\frac{3}{4}$ of a box of 12 eggs is 9 eggs.

Lulu uses 9 eggs to make the cakes.

Practice

1 Draw ☐ to help you find part of the set.

(a)
$\frac{2}{5}$ of 10 apricots = ☐ apricots

(b)
$\frac{2}{3}$ of 18 flowers = ☐ flowers

(c)
$\frac{5}{6}$ of 30 tomatoes = ☐ tomatoes

(d)
$\frac{3}{4}$ of 36 books = ☐ books

2 Fill in the blanks.

(a) $\frac{2}{3}$ of 12 = ☐

(b) $\frac{3}{4}$ of 12 = ☐

(c) $\frac{4}{5}$ of 20 = ☐

(d) $\frac{5}{6}$ of 24 = ☐

Sharing 1

Lesson 17

Starter

How can we share 1 bar of chocolate between more than 1 person?

Example

Two friends share the chocolate.

$1 \div 2 = \frac{1}{2}$

Three friends share the chocolate.

$1 \div 3 = \frac{1}{3}$

Four friends share the chocolate.

$1 \div 4 = \frac{1}{4}$

Practice

1 Divide.

(a) $1 \div 5 = \boxed{}$

(b) $1 \div 7 = \boxed{}$

(c) $1 \div 9 = \boxed{}$

(d) $1 \div 10 = \boxed{}$

(e) $1 \div 12 = \boxed{}$

(f) $1 \div 20 = \boxed{}$

2 Fill in the blanks.

(a) $1 \div \boxed{} = \frac{1}{2}$

(b) $2 \div \boxed{} = 1$

(c) $\boxed{} \div 6 = \frac{1}{6}$

Sharing More Than 1

Lesson 18

Starter

How can we share 2 fruit strips between 3 children?

Example

This is 1.

Cut each fruit strip into thirds.

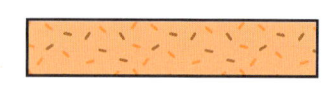

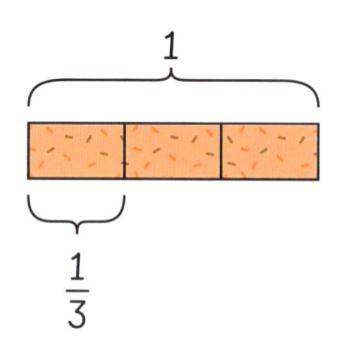

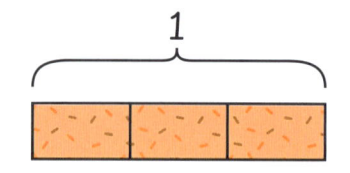

1

$\frac{1}{3}$

Each piece is $\frac{1}{3}$.

Each child receives 2 pieces or $\frac{2}{3}$ of a fruit strip.

$\frac{1}{3} + \frac{1}{3} = \frac{2}{3}$

$2 \div 3 = \frac{2}{3}$

When we divide 2 whole fruit strips between 3 children, each child gets $\frac{2}{3}$ of a fruit strip.

Practice

Divide.

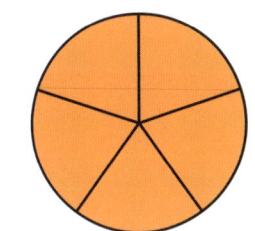

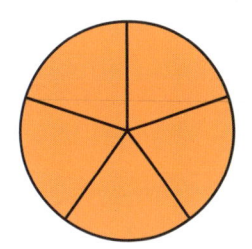

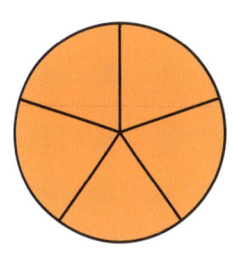

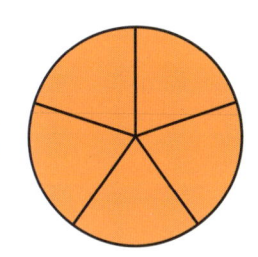

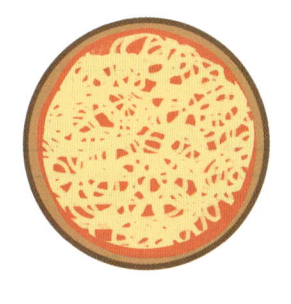

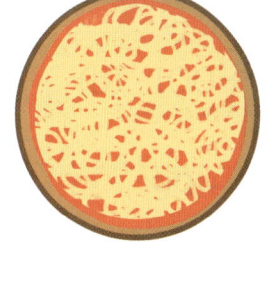

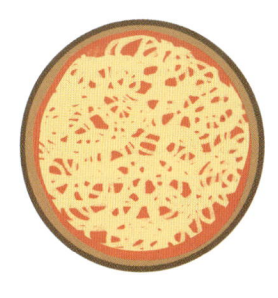

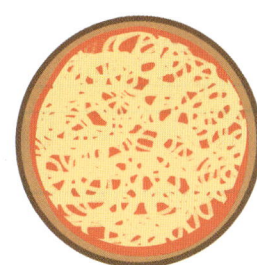

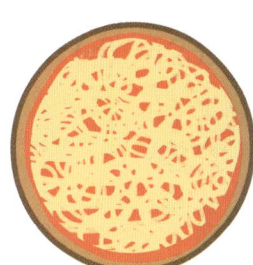

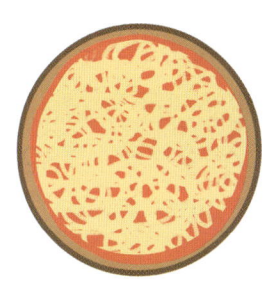

1 3 ÷ 4 =

2 4 ÷ 5 =

3 6 ÷ 7 =

Sharing More Than 1 Using Improper Fractions

Lesson 19

Starter

Lulu needs to cut the sushi rolls so there is an equal amount on each plate.

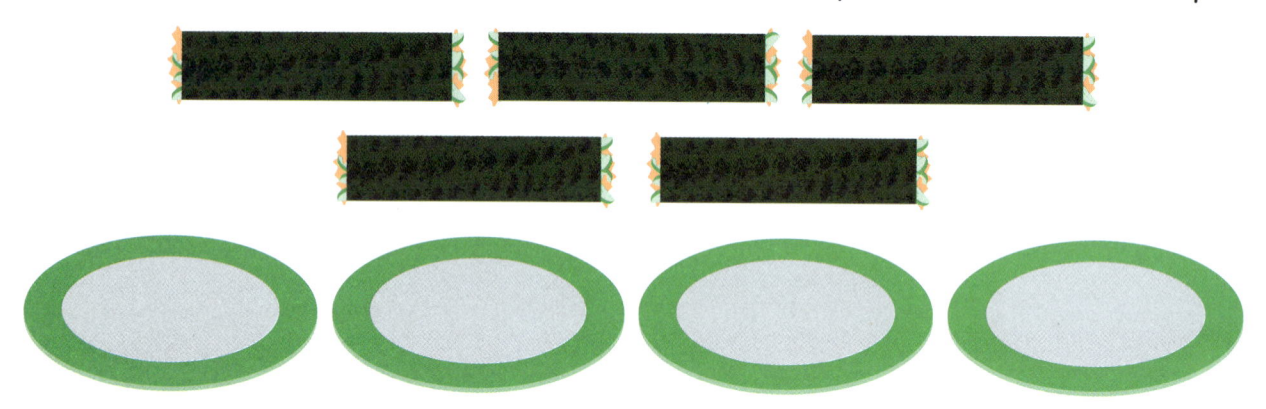

How much sushi roll will be on each plate?

Example

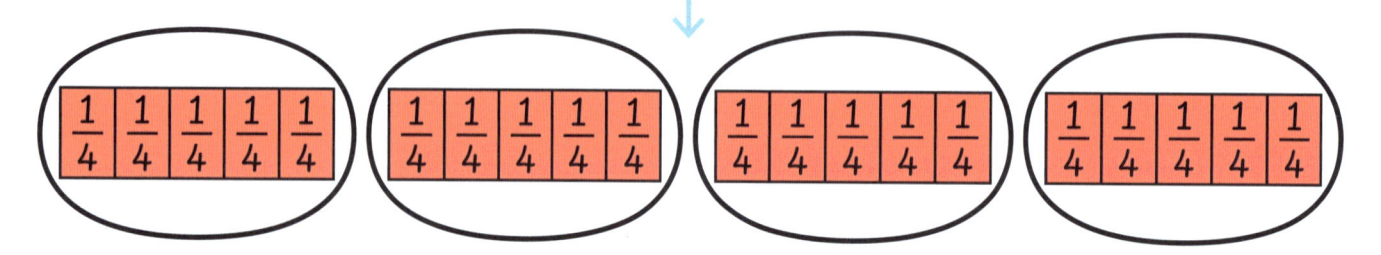

Each whole roll is shared equally between 4 plates.

$1 \div 4 = \frac{1}{4}$

Each roll is cut into quarters.

Five whole rolls are shared equally between 4 plates.

$5 \div 4 = \frac{5}{4}$

Each plate will have 5 quarters or $\frac{5}{4}$ of sushi roll on it.

20 quarters ÷ 4 = 5 quarters

When the numerator of a fraction is greater than or equal to the denominator, we call it an improper fraction.

Practice

Divide.

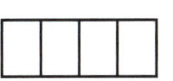

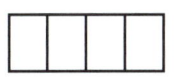

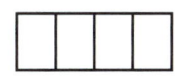

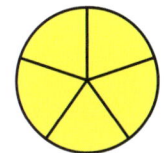

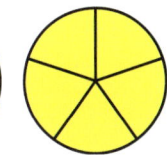

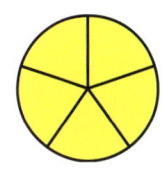

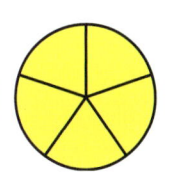

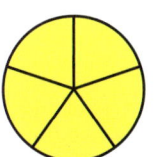

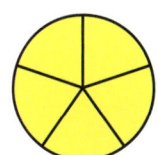

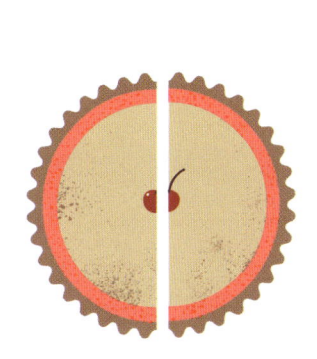

1. $5 \div 4 =$ ☐

2. $6 \div 5 =$ ☐

3. $5 \div 2 =$ ☐

Review and Challenge

1 Add.

(a) $\dfrac{2}{7} + \dfrac{4}{7} = \square$

(b) $\dfrac{4}{9} + \dfrac{5}{9} = \square$

(c) $\dfrac{5}{11} + \dfrac{5}{11} = \square$

(d) $\dfrac{6}{12} + \dfrac{5}{12} = \square$

2 Find all the pairs of tenths that make 1.

$\square + \square$, $\square + \square$, $\square + \square$,

$\square + \square$, $\square + \square$

3 Subtract.

(a) $\dfrac{6}{7} - \dfrac{1}{7} = \square$

(b) $\dfrac{8}{9} - \dfrac{3}{9} = \square$

(c) $\dfrac{10}{11} - \dfrac{3}{11} = \square$

(d) $\dfrac{4}{5} - \dfrac{4}{5} = \square$

4 Find the first 5 equivalent fractions for each of these fractions.

(a) $\dfrac{1}{3} = \square = \square = \square = \square = \square$

(b) $\dfrac{1}{5} = \square = \square = \square = \square = \square$

5 Subtract.

(a) $1 - \dfrac{2}{5} = \square$

(b) $1 - \dfrac{8}{10} = \square$

(c) $1 - \dfrac{7}{8} = \square$

(d) $1 - \dfrac{9}{11} = \square$

6 Write each fraction in its simplest form.

(a) $\dfrac{6}{8} = \square$ (b) $\dfrac{10}{15} = \square$ (c) $\dfrac{6}{10} = \square$

(d) $\dfrac{15}{25} = \square$ (e) $\dfrac{12}{18} = \square$ (f) $\dfrac{10}{24} = \square$

7 Circle the greater fraction.

(a) $\dfrac{3}{4}$ $\dfrac{3}{5}$

(b) $\dfrac{6}{7}$ $\dfrac{7}{8}$ (c) $\dfrac{2}{3}$ $\dfrac{3}{4}$

8 Add and simplify.

(a) $\dfrac{1}{8} + \dfrac{5}{8} = \square = \square$ (b) $\dfrac{1}{10} + \dfrac{7}{10} = \square = \square$

(c) $\dfrac{1}{12} + \dfrac{11}{12} = \square = \square$ (d) $\dfrac{2}{9} + \dfrac{4}{9} = \square = \square$

9 Subtract and simplify.

(a) $\dfrac{5}{8} - \dfrac{1}{8} = \boxed{} = \boxed{}$

(b) $\dfrac{7}{10} - \dfrac{1}{10} = \boxed{} = \boxed{}$

(c) $\dfrac{11}{12} - \dfrac{1}{12} = \boxed{} = \boxed{}$

(d) $\dfrac{5}{9} - \dfrac{2}{9} = \boxed{} = \boxed{}$

10 8 children share 5 sandwiches.
What fraction of a sandwich does each of them get?

Each child gets $\boxed{}$ of a sandwich.

11 5 children share 8 sandwiches.
What fraction of the sandwiches does each of them get?

Each child gets $\boxed{}$ sandwiches.

12 A baker makes a batch of pies.

He sells $\frac{4}{9}$ of them in the morning and $\frac{2}{9}$ of them in the afternoon.

What fraction of the total batch is left over?
Give your answer in its simplest form.

☐ of the total batch is left over.

13 Elliott bakes 36 cookies. He eats $\frac{1}{6}$ of the cookies and gives $\frac{1}{3}$ of the total amount of cookies to his friends.

How many cookies does Elliott have left?

Elliott has ☐ cookies left.

14 Ravi was on vacation for $\frac{1}{4}$ of the days in February.
For how many days was Ravi on vacation?

Ravi was on vacation for ☐ days.

Answers

Page 5   1 (a) $\frac{1}{10}$ (b) $\frac{5}{10}$ 2 (a) $\frac{4}{10}$ (b) $\frac{4}{10}$ (c) $\frac{5}{10}$ OR $\frac{1}{2}$ (d) $\frac{10}{10}$ OR 1 (e) $\frac{3}{10}$ (f) $\frac{3}{10}$ (g) $\frac{5}{10}$ OR $\frac{1}{2}$

3 Boxed: $\frac{3}{10}, \frac{4}{10}, \frac{6}{10}, \frac{7}{10}, \frac{9}{10}$ on number line from 0 to 1.

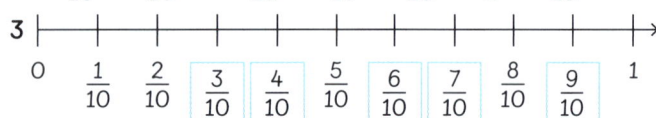

Page 7   1 (a) $\frac{1}{5}+\frac{3}{5}=\frac{4}{5}$ (b) $\frac{2}{5}+\frac{2}{5}=\frac{4}{5}$ (c) $\frac{1}{9}+\frac{7}{9}=\frac{8}{9}$ (d) $\frac{2}{7}+\frac{2}{7}=\frac{4}{7}$ (e) $\frac{1}{4}+\frac{3}{4}=\frac{4}{4}$ OR 1 (f) $\frac{3}{6}+\frac{3}{6}=\frac{6}{6}$ OR 1

2 (a–d) Answers will vary.   3 (a) $\frac{1}{4}+\frac{1}{4}+\frac{1}{4}=\frac{3}{4}$ (b) $\frac{1}{3}+\frac{1}{3}+\frac{1}{3}=\frac{3}{3}$ OR 1 (c) $\frac{1}{5}+\frac{2}{5}+\frac{1}{5}=\frac{4}{5}$ (d) $\frac{1}{7}+\frac{2}{7}+\frac{3}{7}=\frac{6}{7}$

Page 9   1 (a) $\frac{1}{5}+\frac{3}{5}=\frac{4}{5}$ (b) $\frac{2}{9}+\frac{5}{9}=\frac{7}{9}$

(c) $\frac{4}{11}$ and $\frac{6}{11}$; $\frac{4}{11}+\frac{6}{11}=\frac{10}{11}$

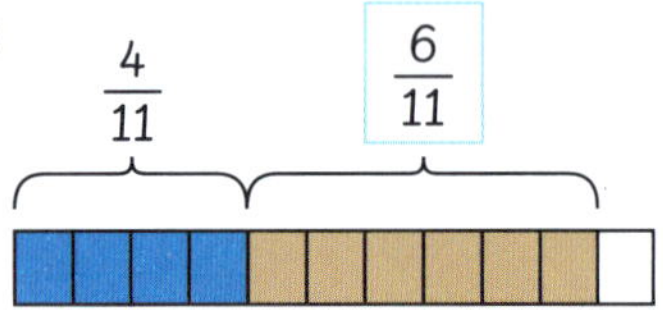

2 (a) $\frac{1}{4}+\frac{2}{4}=\frac{3}{4}$ (b) $\frac{2}{9}+\frac{4}{9}=\frac{6}{9}$ OR $\frac{2}{3}$ (c) $\frac{1}{6}+\frac{5}{6}=\frac{6}{6}$ OR 1 (d) $\frac{1}{15}+\frac{4}{15}=\frac{5}{15}$ OR $\frac{1}{3}$ (e) $\frac{3}{7}+\frac{2}{7}=\frac{5}{7}$ (f) $\frac{4}{15}+\frac{7}{15}=\frac{11}{15}$

Page 11   1 Matching bars to fractions.

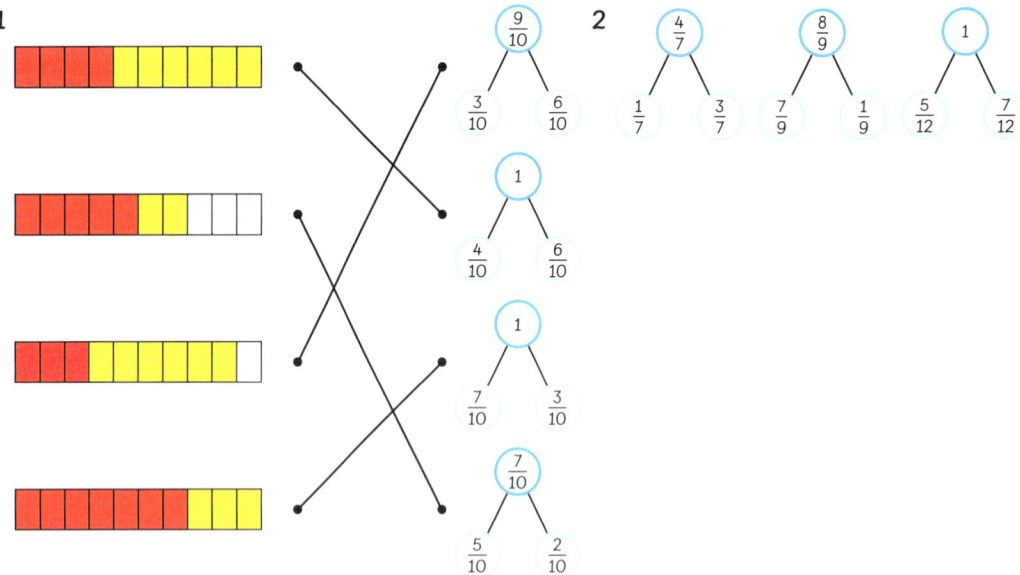

2 $\frac{9}{10}$: $\frac{3}{10}, \frac{6}{10}$; $\frac{4}{7}$: $\frac{1}{7}, \frac{3}{7}$; $\frac{8}{9}$: $\frac{7}{9}, \frac{1}{9}$; 1: $\frac{5}{12}, \frac{7}{12}$; 1: $\frac{4}{10}, \frac{6}{10}$; 1: $\frac{7}{10}, \frac{3}{10}$; $\frac{7}{10}$: $\frac{5}{10}, \frac{2}{10}$

Page 13   1 (a) $\frac{3}{5}-\frac{1}{5}=\frac{2}{5}$ (b) $\frac{5}{8}-\frac{2}{8}=\frac{3}{8}$ (c) $\frac{4}{7}-\frac{3}{7}=\frac{1}{7}$ (d) $\frac{7}{12}-\frac{3}{12}=\frac{4}{12}$ OR $\frac{1}{3}$ 2 Charles has $\frac{1}{4}$ of the money he started with left.

Page 15   1 (a) $\frac{3}{12}$ (b) $\frac{4}{16}$ OR $\frac{1}{4}$ 2 $\frac{1}{3}=\frac{4}{12}$, $\frac{1}{4}=\frac{3}{12}$, $\frac{1}{5}=\frac{2}{10}$ 3 Oak's slices were $\frac{3}{6}$ of a pizza, Ruby's slices were $\frac{4}{8}$ of a pizza, and Holly's slices were $\frac{2}{4}$ of a pizza.

Page 17   1 $\frac{1}{3}$ at $\frac{2}{6}$; $\frac{1}{2}$ at $\frac{3}{6}$ on number line 0 to 1 in sixths.   2 $\frac{1}{4}$ at $\frac{2}{8}$; $\frac{3}{6}$ at $\frac{4}{8}$ on number line 0 to 1 in eighths.

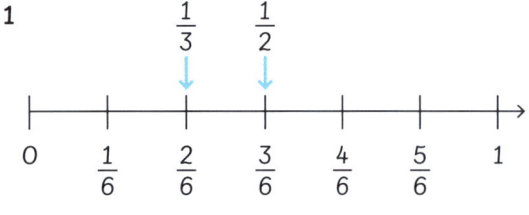

46

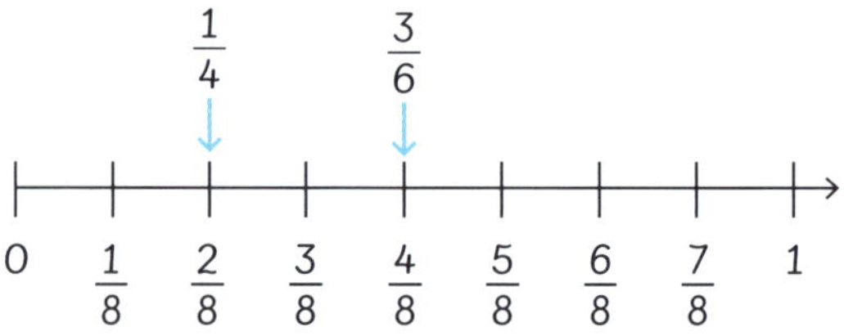

Page 19 1 (a) $\frac{3}{5}=\frac{6}{10}$ (b) $\frac{3}{4}=\frac{6}{8}$ (c) $\frac{2}{7}=\frac{4}{14}$ (d) $\frac{5}{6}=\frac{10}{12}$

2 (a) × 2 ; $\frac{3}{4}=\frac{6}{8}$; × 2 (b) × 3 ; $\frac{2}{5}=\frac{6}{15}$; × 3

Page 21 1 (a) $\frac{1}{2}=\frac{4}{8}$; answers will vary. For example:

(b) $\frac{3}{4}=\frac{6}{8}$; answers will vary. For example:

2 (a) × 2 ; $\frac{1}{5}=\frac{2}{10}$; × 2 (b) × 3 ; $\frac{3}{4}=\frac{9}{12}$; × 3

Page 23 1 (a) × 5 ; $\frac{2}{3}=\frac{10}{15}$; × 5 (b) × 5 ; $\frac{5}{7}=\frac{25}{35}$; × 5 (c) ÷ 4 ; $\frac{8}{12}=\frac{2}{3}$; ÷ 4 (d) ÷ 3 ; $\frac{9}{15}=\frac{3}{5}$; ÷ 3

2 (a) $\frac{15}{25}=\frac{3}{5}$ (b) $\frac{15}{50}=\frac{3}{10}$ (c) $\frac{5}{15}=\frac{1}{3}$ (d) $\frac{50}{60}=\frac{5}{6}$ (e) $\frac{12}{16}=\frac{3}{4}$ (f) $\frac{8}{24}=\frac{1}{3}$

Page 25 1 (a) $\frac{1}{5}$ is greater than $\frac{1}{7}$. (b) $\frac{1}{11}$ is smaller than $\frac{1}{9}$. 2 (a) $\frac{1}{8}<\frac{1}{5}$ (b) $\frac{1}{2}>\frac{1}{10}$ (c) $\frac{1}{3}>\frac{1}{6}$ (d) $\frac{1}{9}<\frac{1}{7}$ (e) $\frac{1}{2}>\frac{1}{3}$ (f) $\frac{1}{5}<\frac{1}{3}$ 3 $\frac{1}{12}, \frac{1}{10}, \frac{1}{5}, \frac{1}{2}$

Page 27 1 (a) $\frac{3}{7}$ is greater than $\frac{3}{10}$. (b) $\frac{7}{10}$ is smaller than $\frac{9}{11}$. 2 (a) $\frac{2}{5}>\frac{2}{7}$ (b) $\frac{3}{7}<\frac{3}{4}$ (c) $\frac{7}{8}>\frac{7}{9}$ (d) $\frac{8}{9}>\frac{7}{8}$ (e) $\frac{10}{11}>\frac{8}{10}$ (f) $\frac{8}{8}=\frac{9}{9}$

Page 29 1 (a) $\frac{7}{8}-\frac{1}{8}=\frac{6}{8}=\frac{3}{4}$ (b) $\frac{7}{8}-\frac{3}{8}=\frac{4}{8}=\frac{1}{2}$ (c) $\frac{9}{10}-\frac{3}{10}=\frac{6}{10}=\frac{3}{5}$ (d) $\frac{5}{9}-\frac{2}{9}=\frac{3}{9}=\frac{1}{3}$

2 (a) $\frac{5}{6}-\frac{2}{6}=\frac{3}{6}=\frac{1}{2}$ (b) $\frac{11}{12}-\frac{2}{12}=\frac{9}{12}=\frac{3}{4}$ (c) $\frac{13}{15}-\frac{8}{15}=\frac{5}{15}=\frac{1}{3}$ (d) $\frac{7}{10}-\frac{2}{10}=\frac{5}{10}=\frac{1}{2}$

3 (a–d) Answers will vary.

Page 31 1 (a) $1-\frac{1}{3}=\frac{2}{3}$ (b) $1-\frac{2}{5}=\frac{3}{5}$ (c) $1-\frac{5}{6}=\frac{1}{6}$ (d) $1-\frac{3}{7}=\frac{4}{7}$ 2 (a) $1-\frac{2}{8}=\frac{6}{8}=\frac{3}{4}$ (b) $1-\frac{3}{9}=\frac{6}{9}=\frac{2}{3}$ (c) $1-\frac{2}{10}=\frac{8}{10}=\frac{4}{5}$ (d) $1-\frac{3}{6}=\frac{3}{6}=\frac{1}{2}$ 3 (a) $1-\frac{2}{6}=\frac{4}{6}=\frac{2}{3}$ (b) $1-\frac{5}{10}=\frac{5}{10}=\frac{1}{2}$ (c) $1-\frac{2}{4}=\frac{1}{2}$

Answers continued

Page 33   **1 (a)** Answers will vary. For example: $\frac{1}{4}$ of 16 cookies = 4 cookies

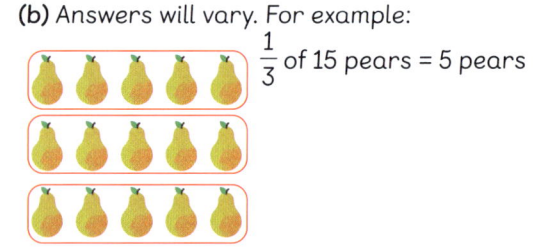

(b) Answers will vary. For example: $\frac{1}{3}$ of 15 pears = 5 pears

2 (a) $\frac{1}{4}$ of 12 pineapples = 3 pineapples   **(b)** $\frac{1}{5}$ of 20 balls = 4 balls   **(c)** $\frac{1}{3}$ of 18 children = 6 children

Page 35   **1 (a)** $\frac{2}{5}$ of 10 apricots = 4 apricots   **(b)** $\frac{2}{3}$ of 18 flowers = 12 flowers

(c) $\frac{5}{6}$ of 30 tomatoes = 25 tomatoes   **(d)** $\frac{3}{4}$ of 36 books = 27 books   **2 (a)** $\frac{2}{3}$ of 12 = 8

(b) $\frac{3}{4}$ of 12 = 9   **(c)** $\frac{4}{5}$ of 20 = 16   **(d)** $\frac{5}{6}$ of 24 = 20

Page 37   **1 (a)** $1 \div 5 = \frac{1}{5}$ **(b)** $1 \div 7 = \frac{1}{7}$ **(c)** $1 \div 9 = \frac{1}{9}$ **(d)** $1 \div 10 = \frac{1}{10}$ **(e)** $1 \div 12 = \frac{1}{12}$ **(f)** $1 \div 20 = \frac{1}{20}$

2 (a) $1 \div 2 = \frac{1}{2}$ **(b)** $2 \div 2 = 1$ **(c)** $1 \div 6 = \frac{1}{6}$

Page 39   **1** $3 \div 4 = \frac{3}{4}$ **2** $4 \div 5 = \frac{4}{5}$ **3** $6 \div 7 = \frac{6}{7}$

Page 41   **1** $5 \div 4 = \frac{5}{4}$ **2** $6 \div 5 = \frac{6}{5}$ **3** $5 \div 2 = \frac{5}{2}$

Page 42   **1 (a)** $\frac{2}{7} + \frac{4}{7} = \frac{6}{7}$ **(b)** $\frac{4}{9} + \frac{5}{9} = \frac{9}{9}$ OR 1   **(c)** $\frac{5}{11} + \frac{5}{11} = \frac{10}{11}$ **(d)** $\frac{6}{12} + \frac{5}{12} = \frac{11}{12}$

2 $\frac{1}{10} + \frac{9}{10}, \frac{2}{10} + \frac{8}{10}, \frac{3}{10} + \frac{7}{10}, \frac{4}{10} + \frac{6}{10}, \frac{5}{10} + \frac{5}{10}$ **3 (a)** $\frac{6}{7} - \frac{1}{7} = \frac{5}{7}$ **(b)** $\frac{8}{9} - \frac{3}{9} = \frac{5}{9}$ **(c)** $\frac{10}{11} - \frac{3}{11} = \frac{7}{11}$

(d) $\frac{4}{5} - \frac{4}{5} = 0$ **4 (a)** $\frac{1}{3} = \frac{2}{6} = \frac{3}{9} = \frac{4}{12} = \frac{5}{15} = \frac{6}{18}$ **(b)** $\frac{1}{5} = \frac{2}{10} = \frac{3}{15} = \frac{4}{20} = \frac{5}{25} = \frac{6}{30}$

Page 43   **5 (a)** $1 - \frac{2}{5} = \frac{3}{5}$ **(b)** $1 - \frac{8}{10} = \frac{2}{10}$ OR $\frac{1}{5}$ **(c)** $1 - \frac{7}{8} = \frac{1}{8}$ **(d)** $1 - \frac{9}{11} = \frac{2}{11}$ **6 (a)** $\frac{6}{8} = \frac{3}{4}$ **(b)** $\frac{10}{15} = \frac{2}{3}$ **(c)** $\frac{6}{10} = \frac{3}{5}$ **(d)** $\frac{15}{25} = \frac{3}{5}$

(e) $\frac{12}{18} = \frac{2}{3}$ **(f)** $\frac{10}{24} = \frac{5}{12}$ **7 (a)** $\frac{3}{4}$ **(b)** $\frac{7}{8}$ **(c)** $\frac{3}{4}$ **8 (a)** $\frac{1}{8} + \frac{5}{8} = \frac{6}{8} = \frac{3}{4}$ **(b)** $\frac{1}{10} + \frac{7}{10} = \frac{8}{10} = \frac{4}{5}$ **(c)** $\frac{1}{12} + \frac{11}{12} = \frac{12}{12} = 1$

(d) $\frac{2}{9} + \frac{4}{9} = \frac{6}{9} = \frac{2}{3}$

Page 44   **9 (a)** $\frac{5}{8} - \frac{1}{8} = \frac{4}{8} = \frac{1}{2}$ **(b)** $\frac{7}{10} - \frac{1}{10} = \frac{6}{10} = \frac{3}{5}$ **(c)** $\frac{11}{12} - \frac{1}{12} = \frac{10}{12} = \frac{5}{6}$ **(d)** $\frac{5}{9} - \frac{2}{9} = \frac{3}{9} = \frac{1}{3}$

10 Each child gets $\frac{5}{8}$ of a sandwich.   **11** Each child gets $1\frac{3}{5}$ sandwiches.

Page 45   **12** $\frac{1}{3}$ of the total batch is left over.   **13** Elliott has 18 cookies left.

14 Ravi was on vacation for 7 days.